Country Cabins
Coloring Book

This Book Belongs To

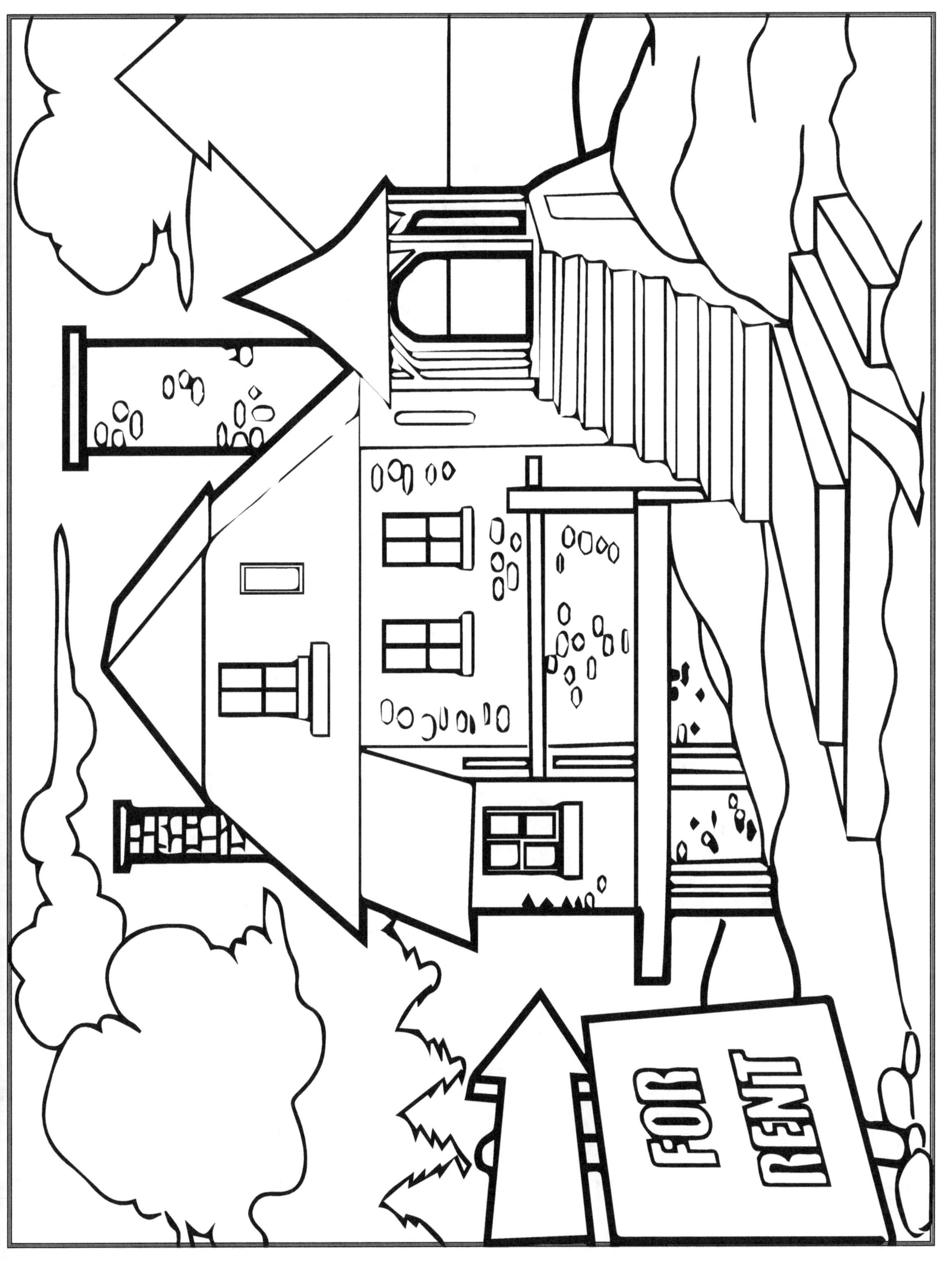

FOR
RENT

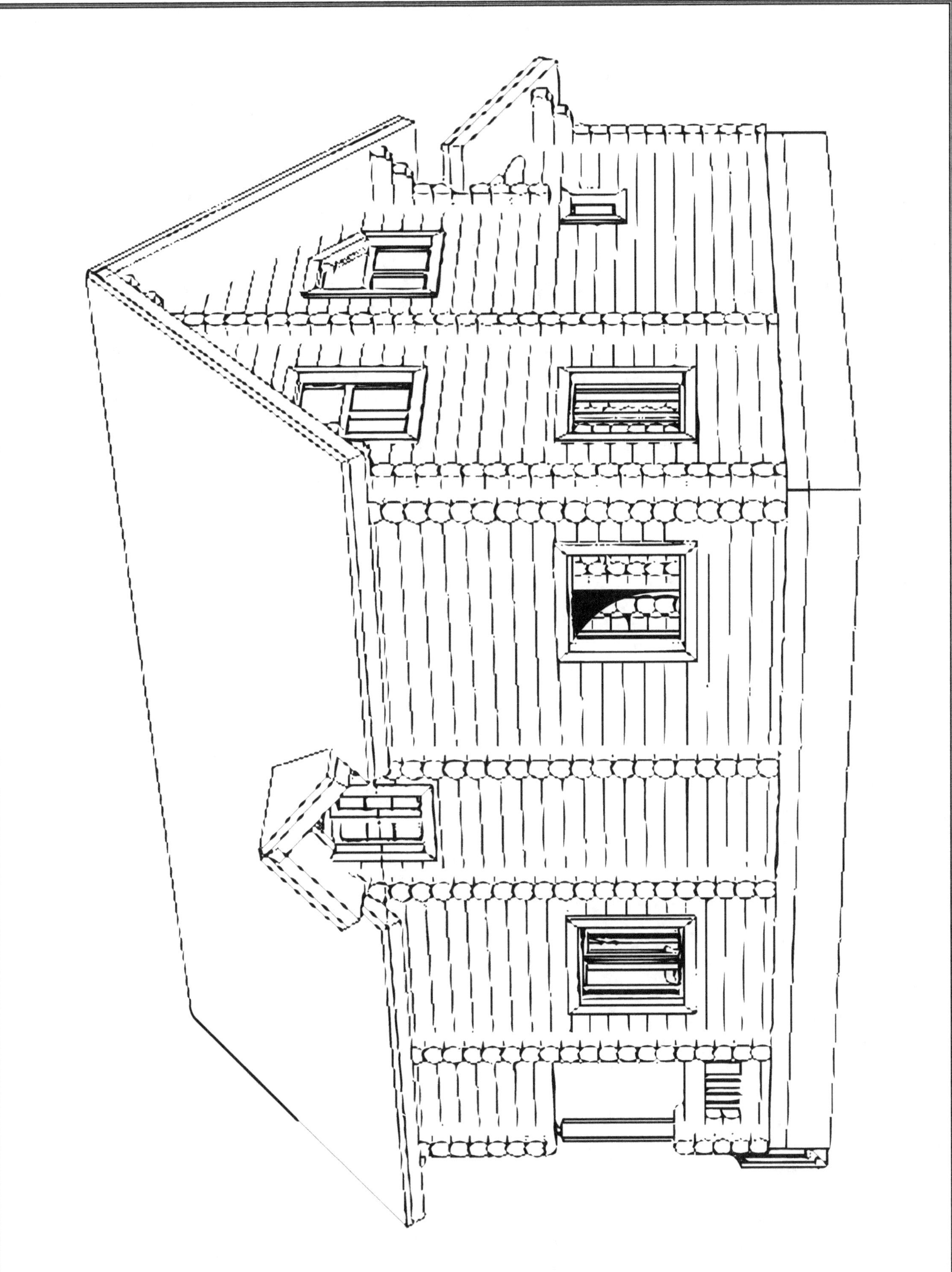

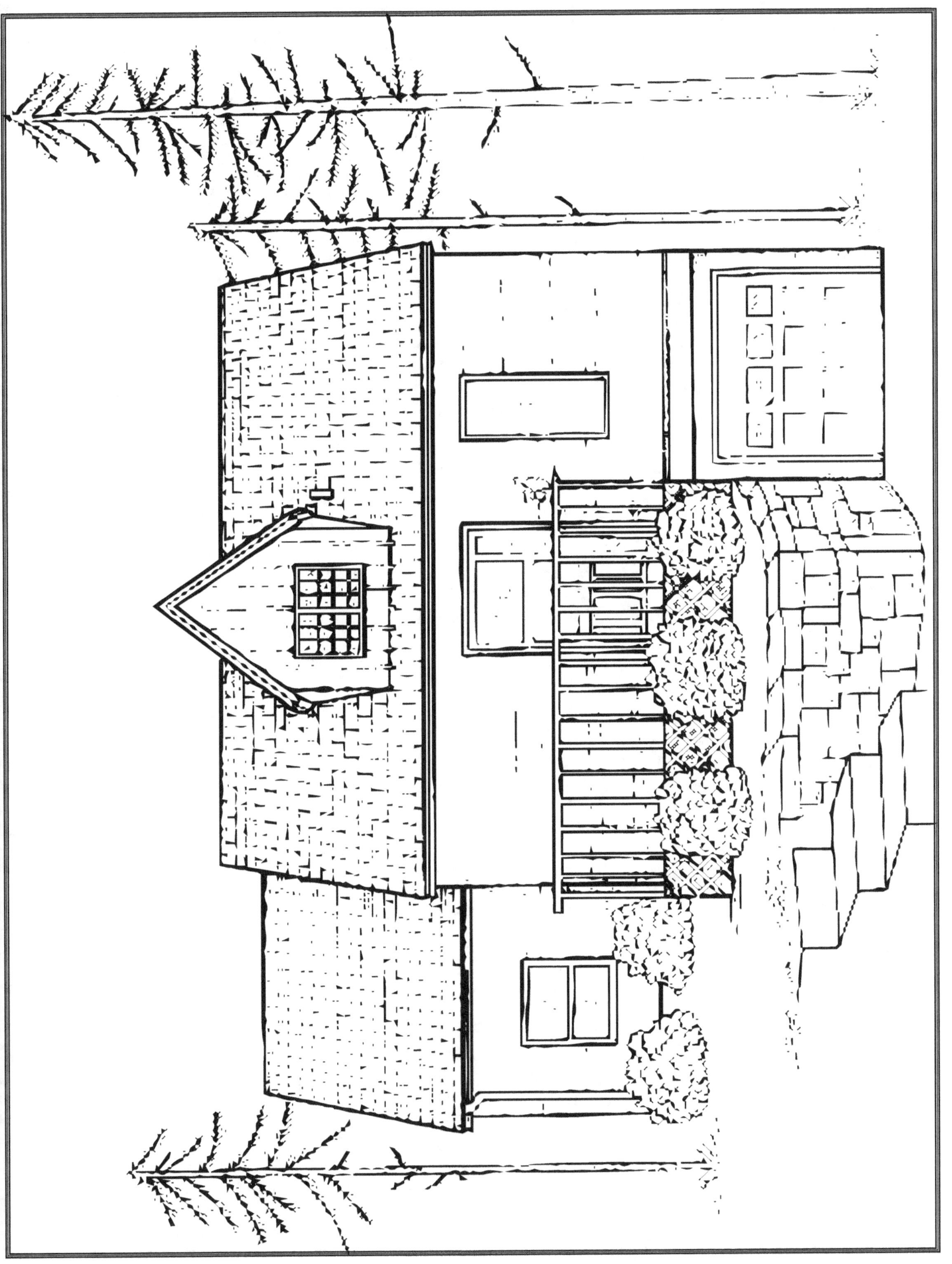

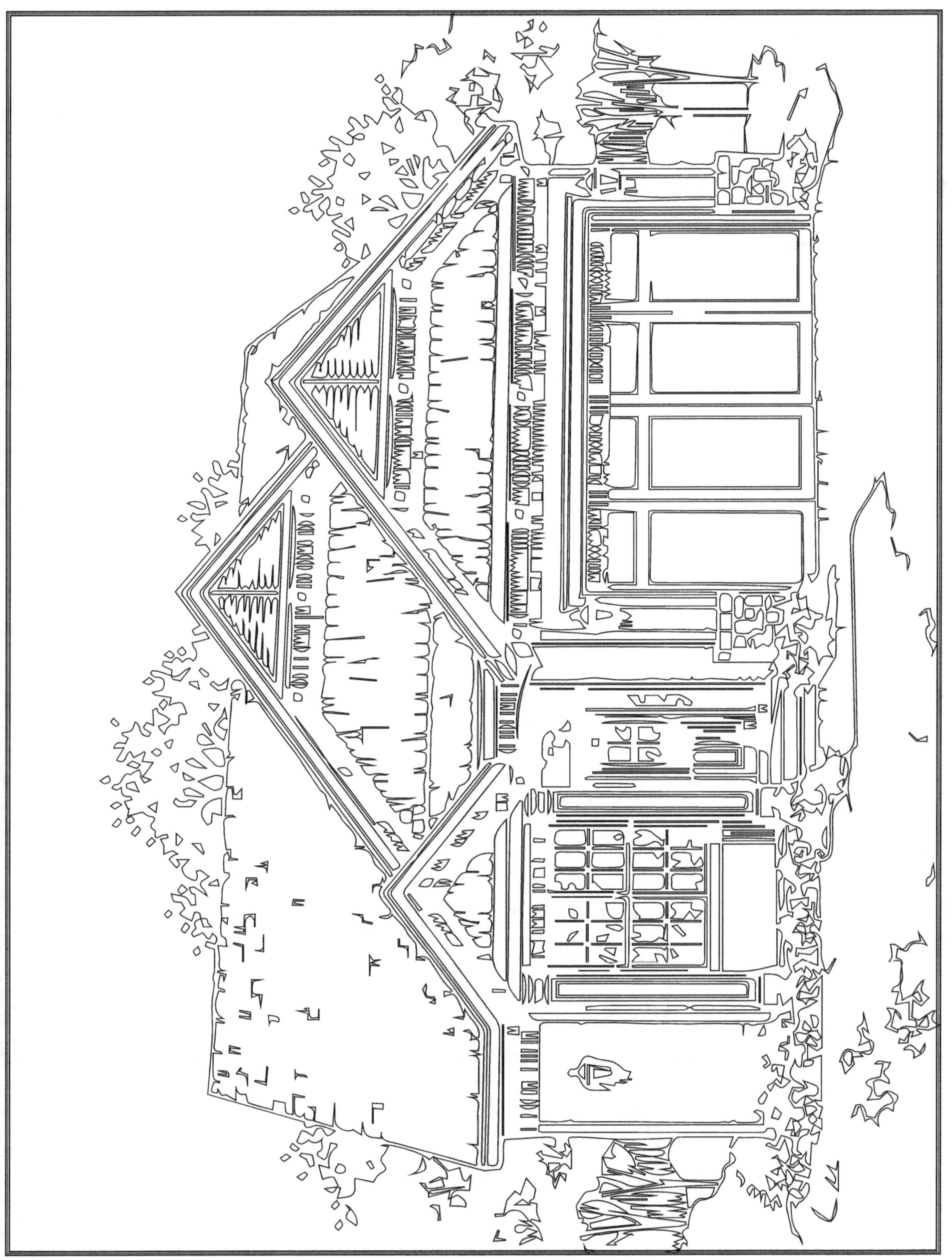

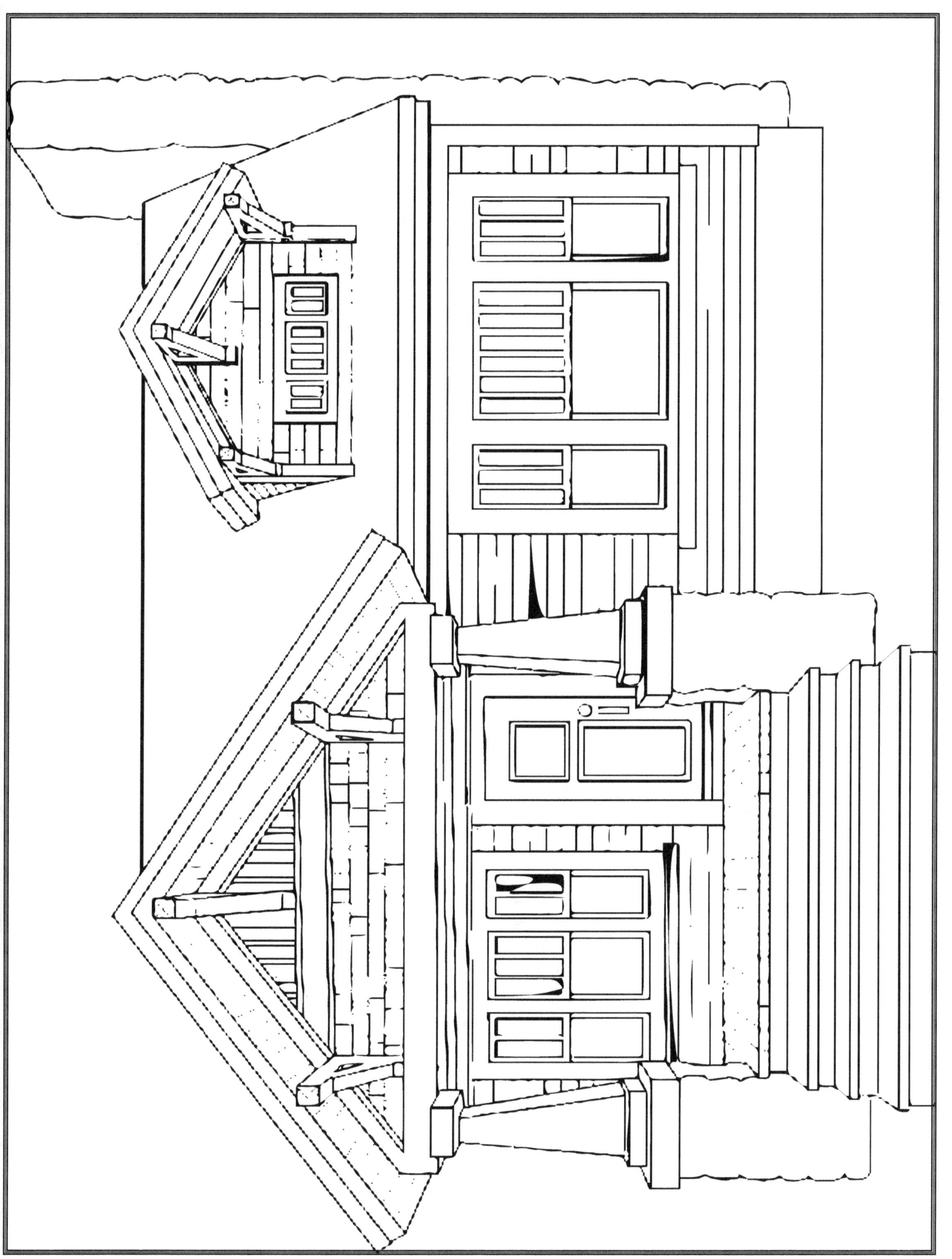

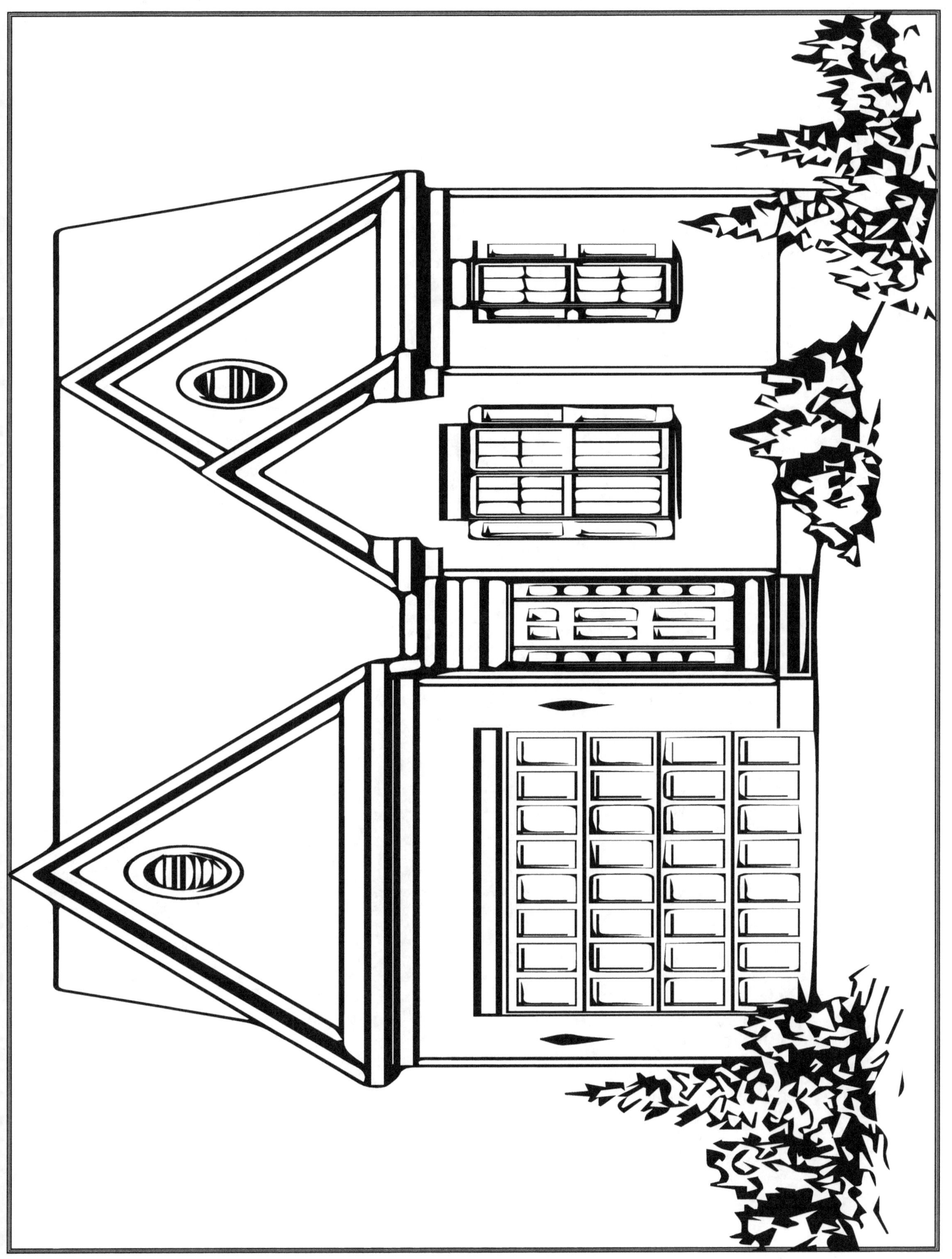

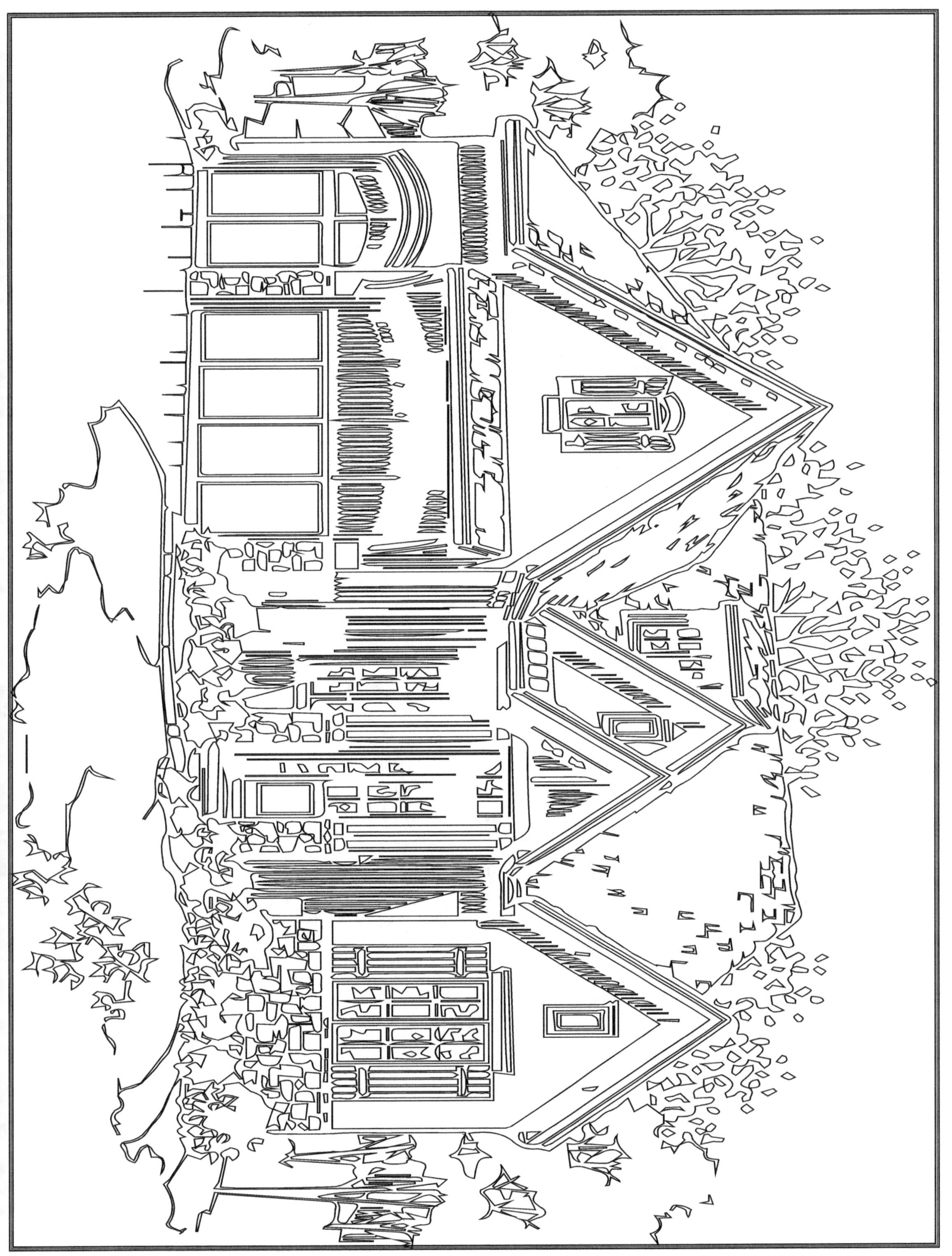

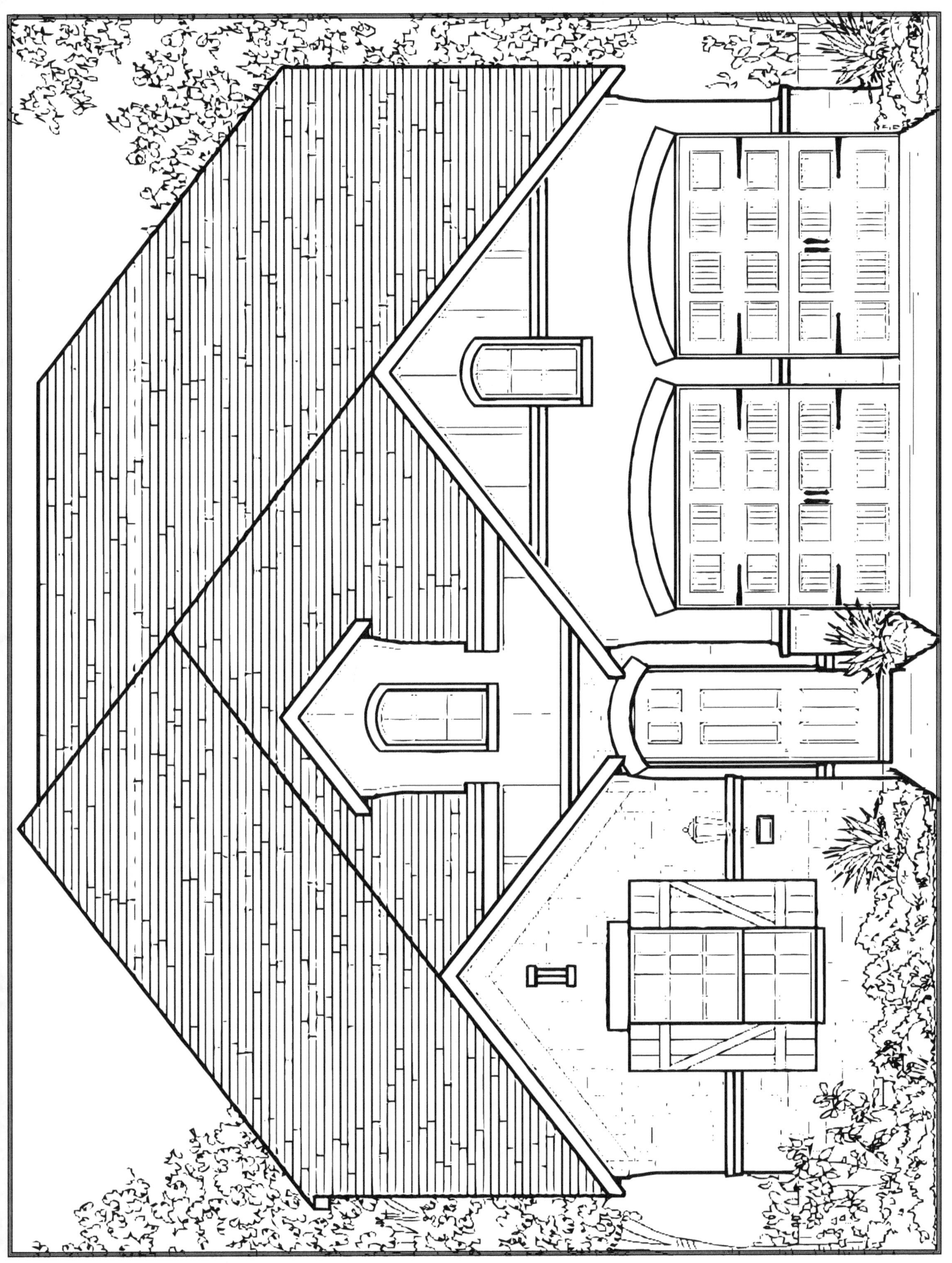

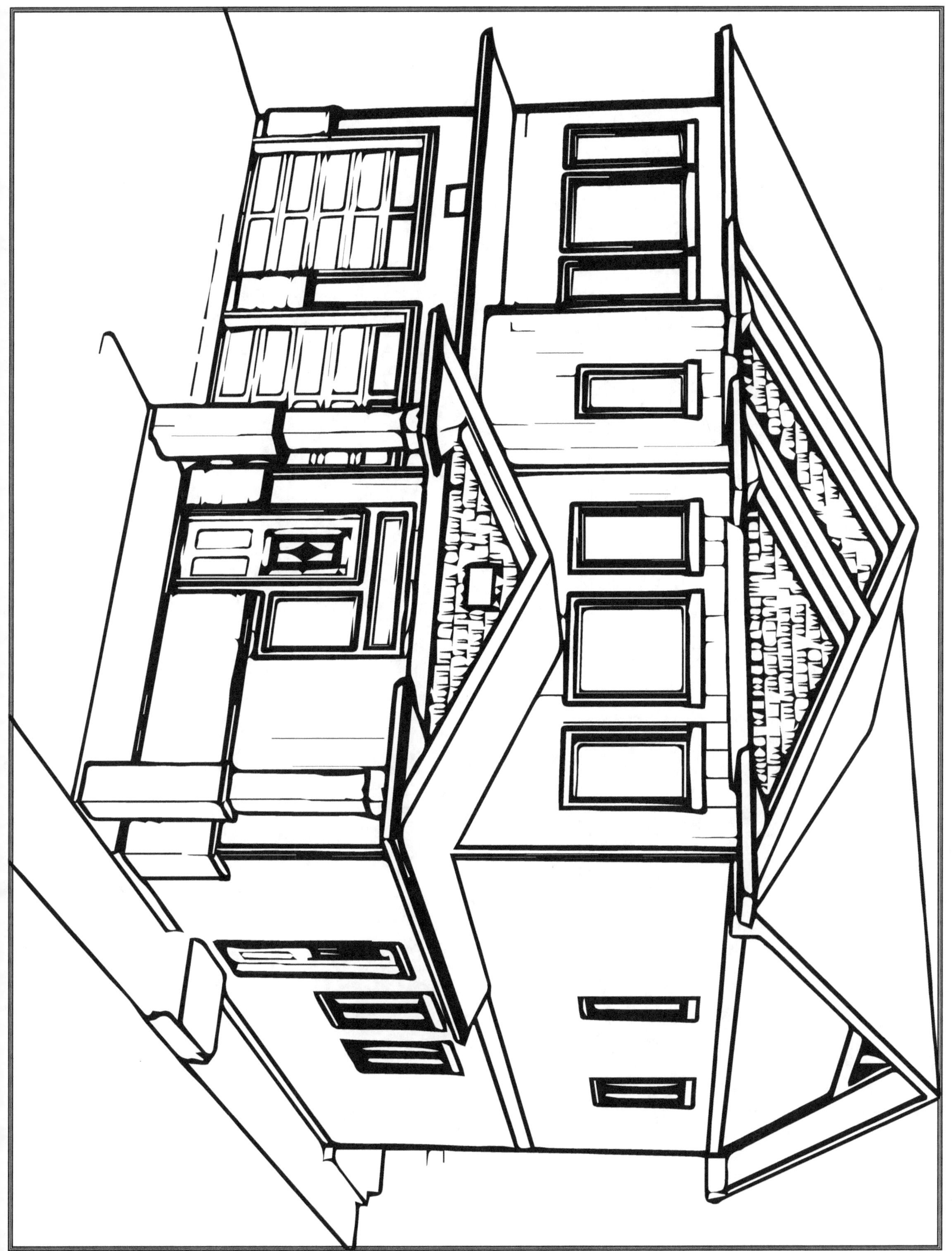

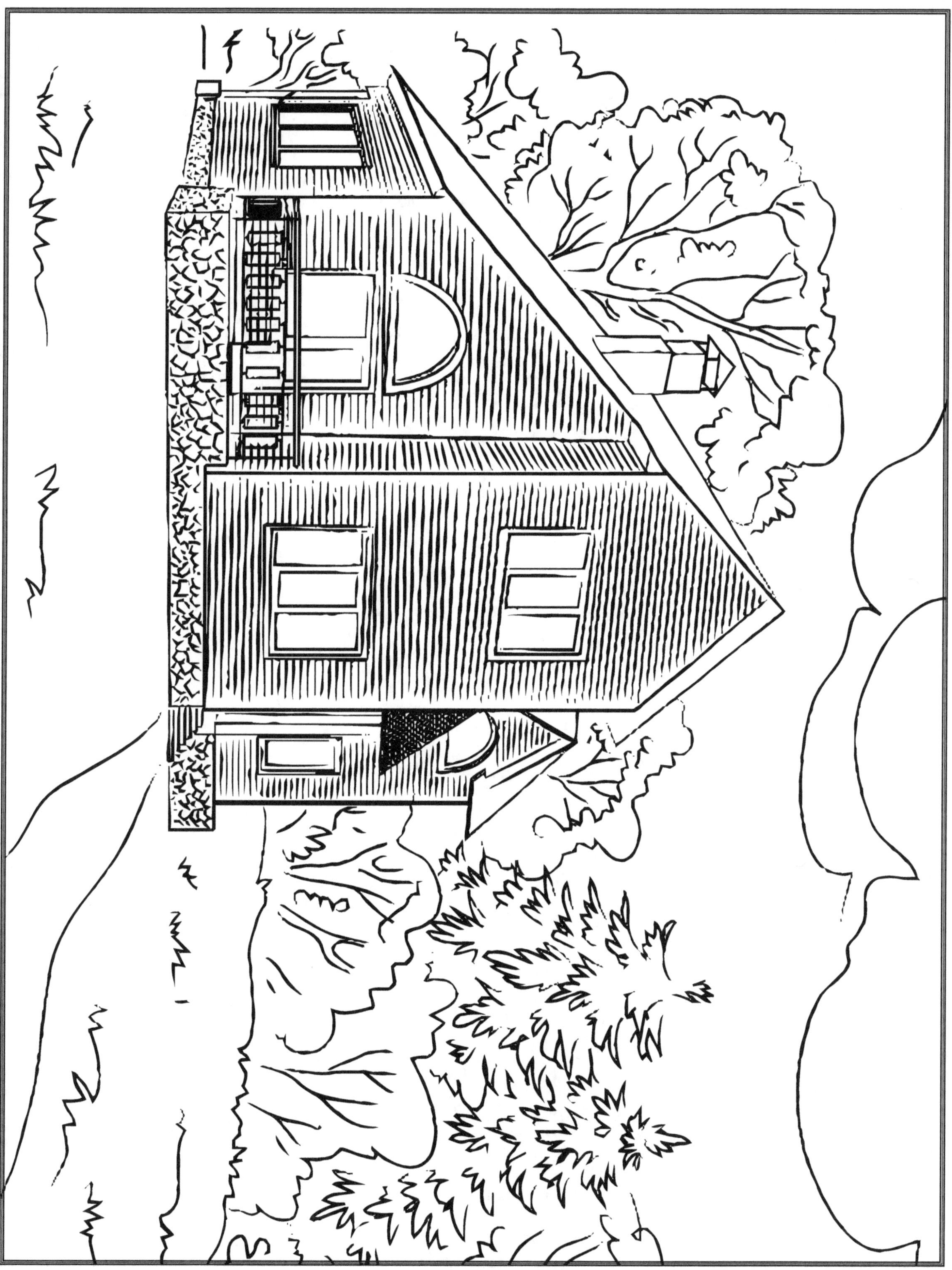

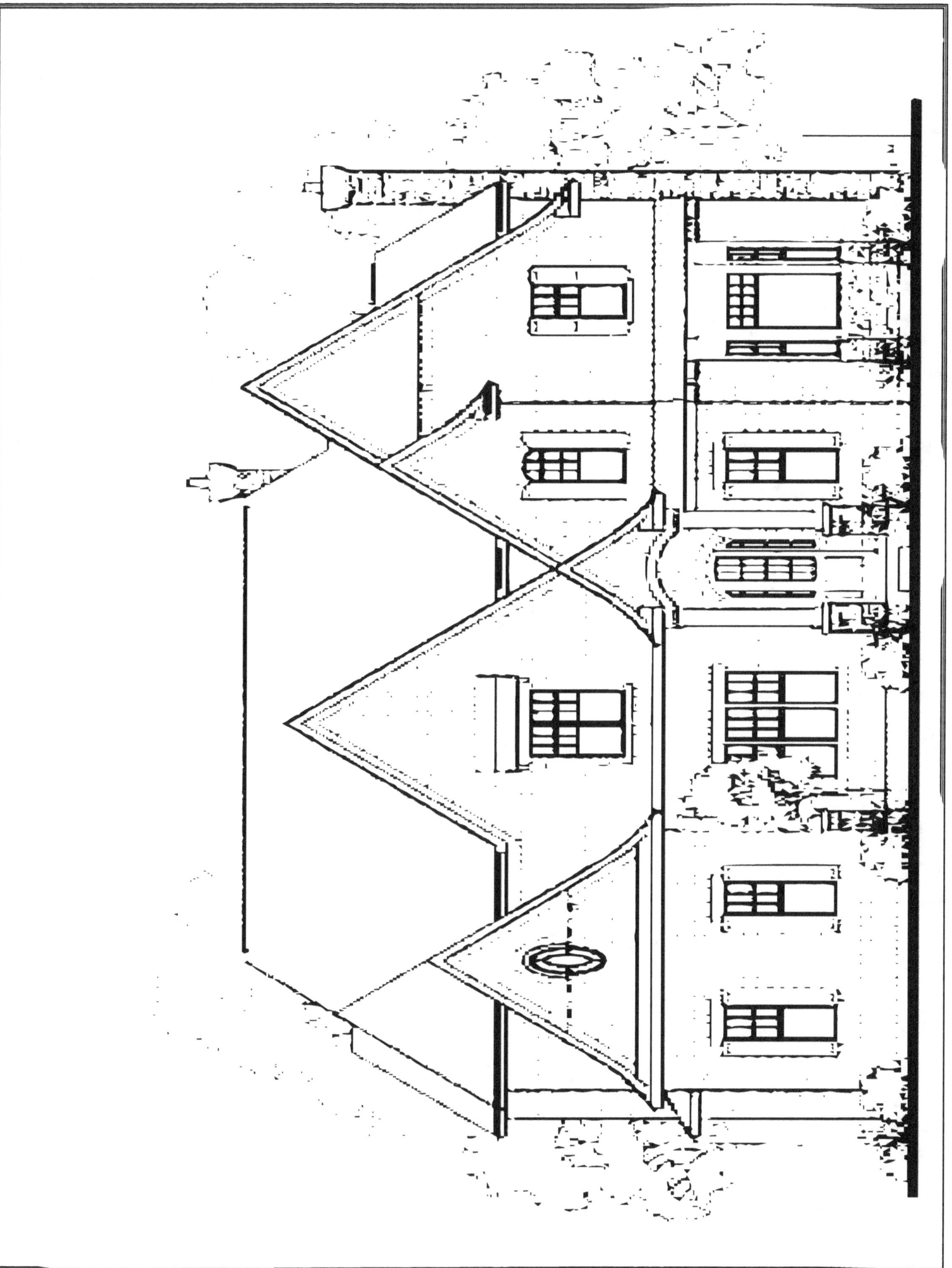

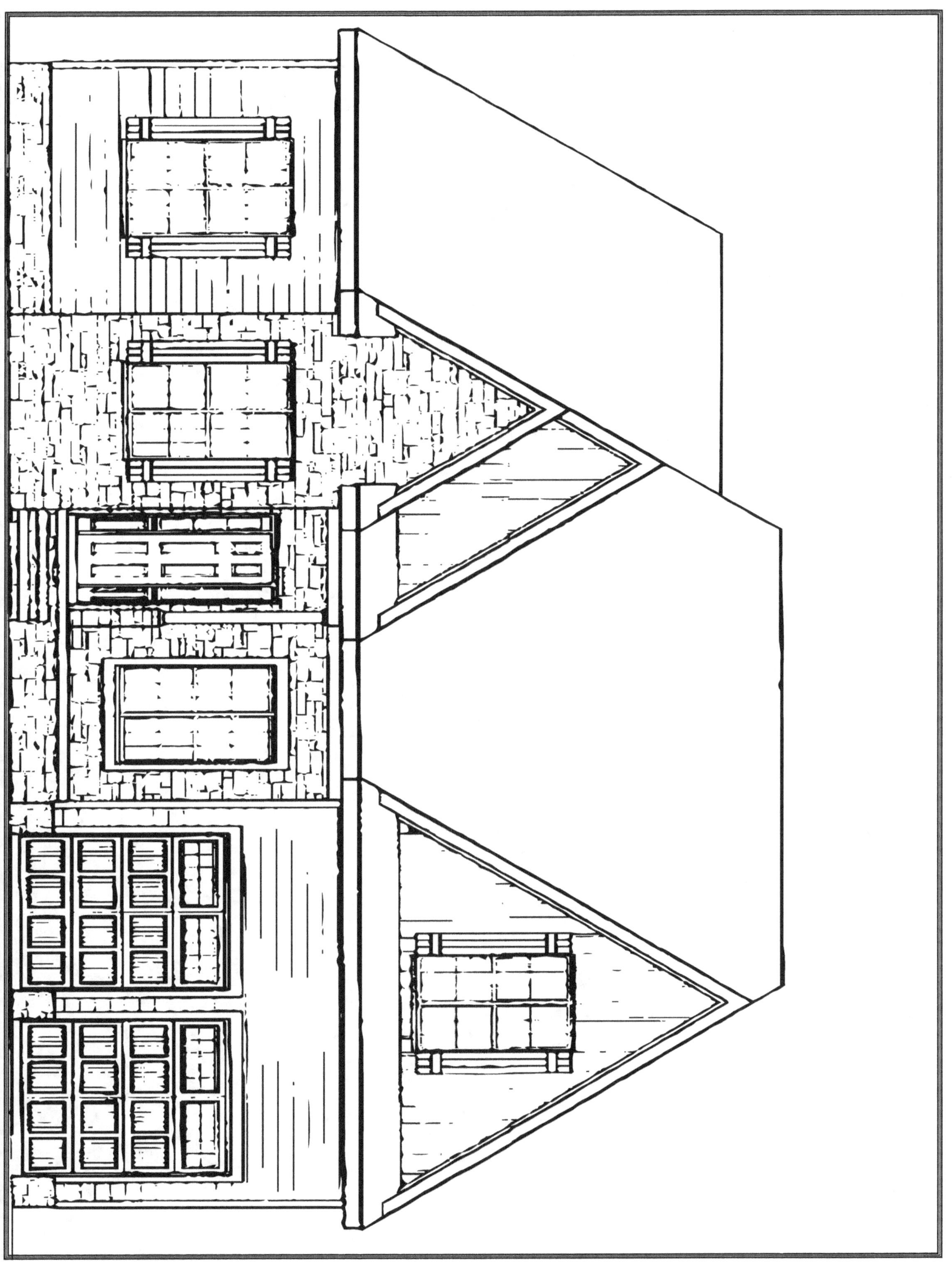

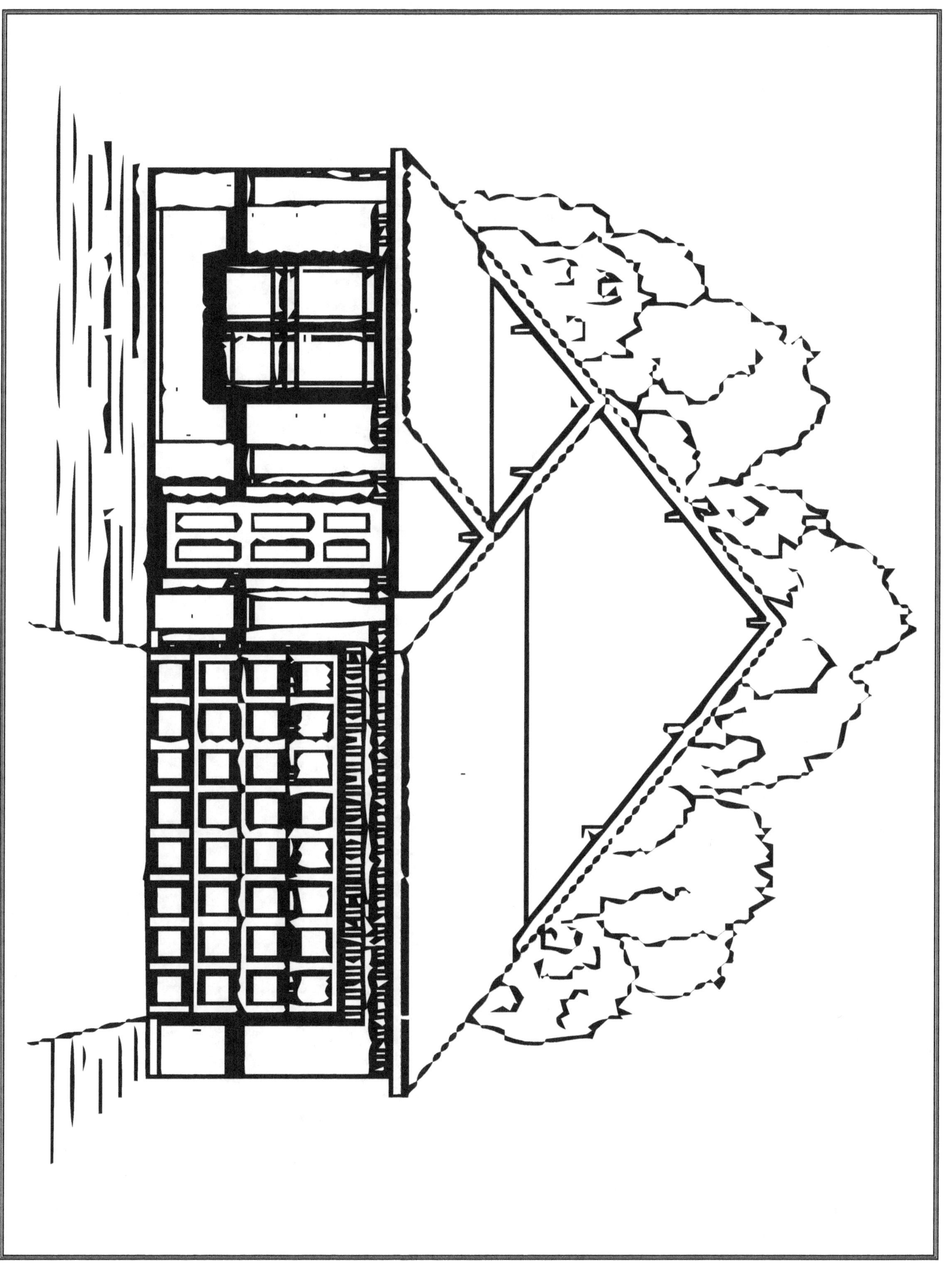

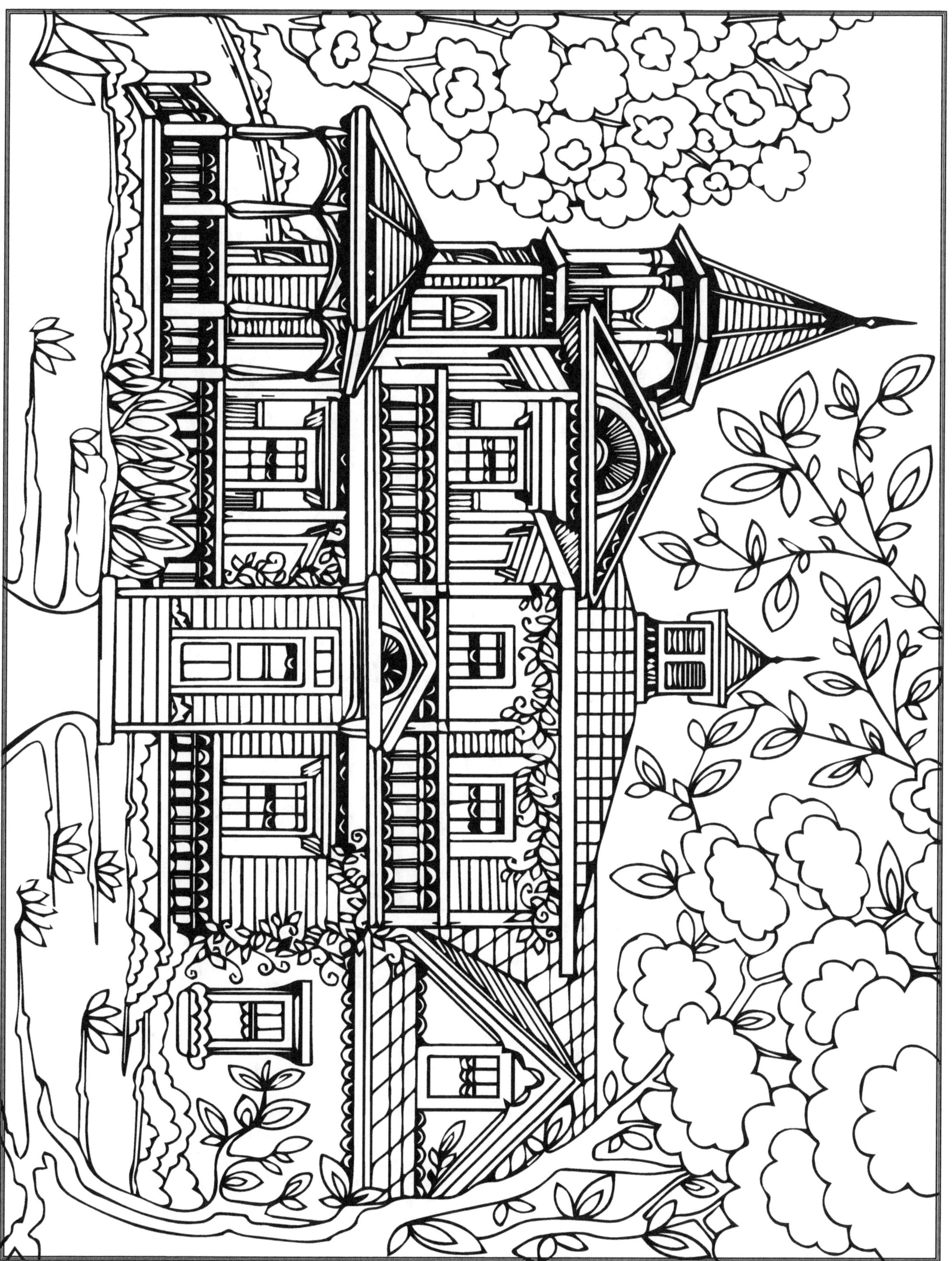

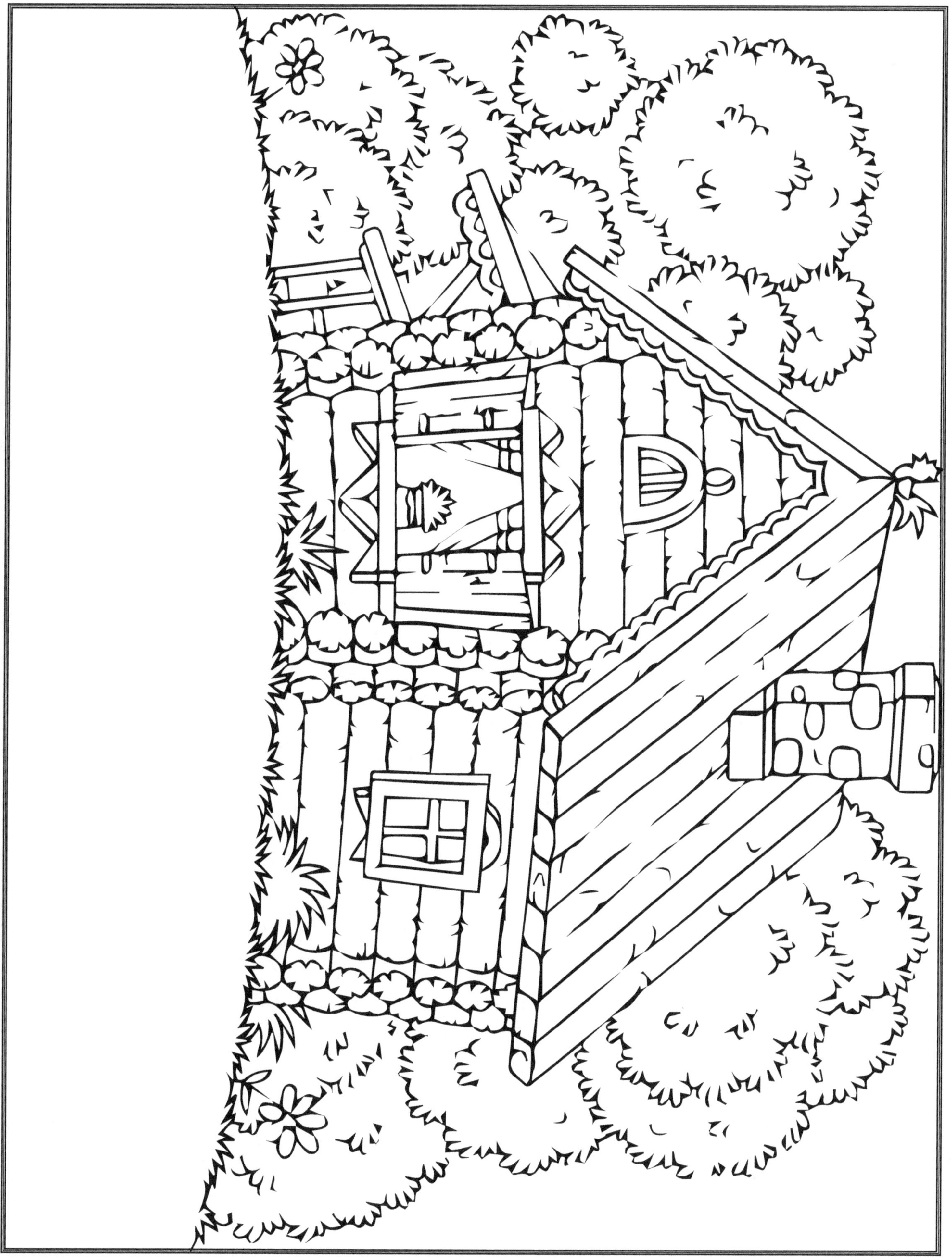

www.ingramcontent.com/pod-product-compliance
Lightning Source LLC
Chambersburg PA
CBHW081419250726
48654CB00013B/1762